No part of this publication may be reproduced in whole or in part, or stored in a retrieval system, or transmitted in any form or by any means, electronic, mechanical, photocopying, recording, or otherwise, without written permission of the publisher.

isbn# 0-7948-0718-6

© 2001 U.S. MINT UNDER LICENSE TO H.E. HARRIS & CO.

MADE IN USA

The Official United States Mint 50 State Quarters™ Handbook is a publication of H.E. Harris & Co., that has been developed by The Jim Henson Company under a license from the United States Mint. The 50 State Quarters, the 50 State Quarters logo, and the official Treasury Department/United States Mint seal are trademarks of the United States Mint. All rights reserved.

Serving the Collector Since 1916

10   9   8   7   6   5   4   3   2   1

FIRST PRINTING

The Official U.S. Mint
Stories of the 1999

H.E. Harris & Co.
Serving the Collector Since 1916

PROGRAM

If you flip over any of the 50 State Quarters™ Program coins, you will see that each has a different state design on its tail side (known as the reverse). In 1997, Congress passed an Act that established the 50 State Quarters™ Program. The program calls for the production of five new quarters every year for ten years. These commemorative quarters honor each state by featuring a symbol of its history, and are issued in the order that the state accepted the U.S. Constitution and entered the Union.

The many changes in the quarter's design are historical firsts, and are especially noteworthy considering how little the quarter has changed since its birth. The first quarter was minted in 1796, and was originally made of silver. The Mint Act of April 2, 1792, called for the quarter design to feature the date the quarter was minted, the word "Liberty," and an image representing liberty. The image chosen was Lady Liberty, a woman in long robes with gently flowing hair. For over 115 years, she represented the idea of liberty on the quarter's front (called the obverse). Although the style of Lady Liberty's dress and hair changed over the years, it was not until George Washington's 200th birthday in 1932 that the first president replaced Liberty on the obverse of the 25 cent coin.

From the beginning of the 50 State Quarters™ Program in 1999, through its end in 2008, the reverse of the coin will change 50 times. Each coin will not only represent a part of our nation's remarkable past, but will also be a piece of history itself.

DELAWARE

Caesar Rodney is honored on the Delaware quarter

Capital: Dover
State Flower: Peach Blossom
State Tree: American Holly
State Bird: Blue Hen Chicken
Land Area: 1,955 sq. mi.
Rank in Size (Land Area): 49th
State Song: "Our Delaware"
Largest City: Wilmington
Statehood Date: December 7, 1787
Nicknames: First State, Diamond State, Blue Hen State, Small Wonder

Delaware was named after an early Virginia colonial governor, Lord De La Warr.

DELAWARE: LIBERTY AND INDEPENDENCE

In the early 1600s, Virginian Samuel Argall was exploring America's northeast coastline when a storm blew him off-course and onto an unknown river. Argall named the river after the first governor of Virginia, Lord de la Warr. The state later took its name from the river.

Delaware also has several nicknames. During the American Revolution, soldiers staged cockfights with blue hen chickens. Entering battle, they would shout, "We're sons of the blue hen and we're game to the end!" It may sound like a silly thing to say, but before long, the soldiers were called "Blue Hen's Chickens"-and eventually Delaware was nicknamed The Blue Hen State.

After the revolution, Delaware picked up a new nickname. Because it was the first colony to unanimously ratify the U.S. Constitution (on December 7, 1787), it is known as "The First State" of the new Federal Union. Later, Thomas Jefferson coined the name "The Diamond State," because he believed Delaware's location (bordered by the Delaware Bay and the Atlantic Ocean, as well as by Maryland, Pennsylvania, and New Jersey) made it as valuable as a jewel.

More recently, Delaware earned the nickname "Small Wonder," because despite its size, it contributes much to the history, industry, and beauty of our nation.

CAESAR RODNEY'S RIDE FOR FREEDOM

If you look at the back of the Delaware quarter, you will see Caesar Rodney astride his horse on his historic ride for independence. His ride took place when the United States was still just a handful of colonies ruled by the British. Colonists who opposed British rule, known as Patriots, wanted to be free to decide all the laws that affected their lives. But colonists called Loyalists (because they remained loyal to the King of England) disagreed. In 1776, delegates from the thirteen colonies met to debate the issue of independence from the English crown. This historic meeting-the Second Continental Congress-determined the fate of our country.

Caesar Rodney was one of three delegates from the small colony of Delaware chosen to participate in the meeting. When the Congress met on July 1, 1776, one Delaware delegate voted in favor of independence, the other against. Rodney was needed to cast the deciding vote, but he was missing! A very busy man (he was the speaker of the State Assembly, a justice to the Supreme Court, and a brigadier general of Delaware's militia), Rodney had been called to Dover on official business a few days before the Continental Congress was to vote. So when his vote was needed in Philadelphia, Caesar Rodney was in Dover, nearly 80 miles away.

As soon as Rodney was called to Philadelphia, he jumped on his horse and rode through the soaking rain of a summer storm. He arrived in Philadelphia on the afternoon of July 2, 1776, just as the debate on independence was drawing to a close. Mud-splattered and weary from his journey, Rodney cast his vote for independence, and for our nation's freedom.

IN THE BEGINNING

Before Delaware was settled by the Swedish in 1638, captured by the Dutch in 1655, and later colonized by the English in 1664, it was inhabited by the Lenni-Lanape and Nanticoke Indians. These Native American tribes lived in bark longhouses and wigwams bordering rivers, and were largely farmers and hunters. For many years the tribes traded with Europeans, but they were gradually pushed westward to Ohio and Kansas, and in 1867, they were forced to relocate to Oklahoma by United States' soldiers.

DO THE FUNKY CHICKEN

There is something about Delaware and that great bird we call the chicken. Not only is Delaware nicknamed The Blue Hen State, but broiler chickens are the state's leading farm product. In 1923, Cecile Steele raised nearly 500 chickens on her farm and started the first Delaware business to sell chickens for food. Today, Delaware is the country's 7th largest producer of broiler chickens, raising 225 million of them a year-an amount almost equal to America's population.

A STAR, AND SOME STRIPES, ARE BORN

Legend has it that the American flag was first raised on Delaware soil at the Battle of Cooch's Bridge in 1777. The first flag was designed according to a resolution passed by the Continental Congress. This Flag Act: "Resolved, That the flag of the United States be made of thirteen stripes, alternate red and white; that the union be thirteen stars, white in a blue field, representing a new Constellation."

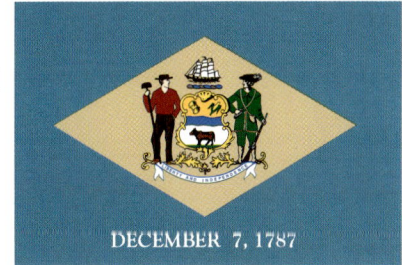

A DATE WITH THE MOON... WHAT TO WEAR?

The big, white space suits worn by American astronauts on the moon were made right here on Earth, in Delaware!

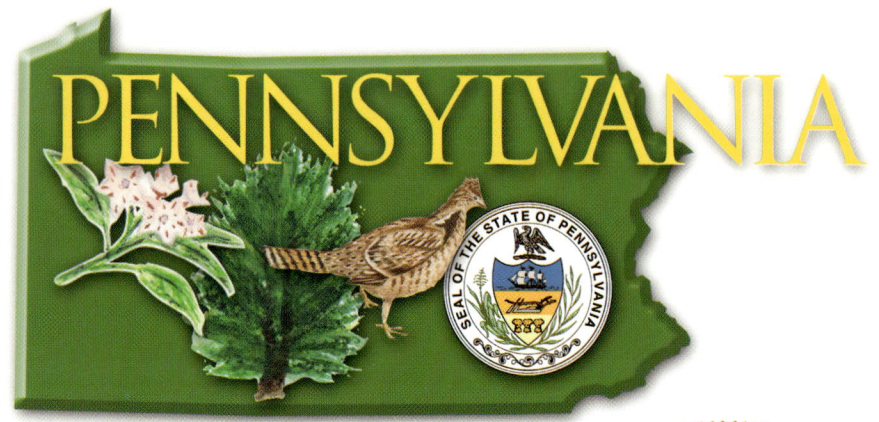

Capital: Harrisburg
State Flower: Mountain Laurel
State Tree: Hemlock
State Bird: Ruffed Grouse
Land Area: 44,820 sq. mi.
Rank in Size (Land Area): 32th
State Song: "Pennsylvania"
Largest City: Philadelphia
Statehood Date: December 12, 1787
Nickname: Keystone State

The commonwealth statue is pictured on the Pennsylvania coin.

Pennsylvania was named in honor of the father of the state's founder, William Penn. The name means "Penn's woods."

PENNSYLVANIA: VIRTUE, LIBERTY & INDEPENDENCE

When William Penn founded the colony of Pennsylvania in 1682, he wanted to name it Sylvania (or "woods"), because of its thick forests and woodlands. But King Charles II of England, who granted the colony to young William, felt it should bear the name of Penn's father. Combining the names, King Charles II dubbed the colony Pennsylvania.

As the colony grew, Pennsylvania became known for its central location between the six colonies to its north and the six to its south. Many people called it "The Keystone State," comparing it to a wedge-shaped stone at the center of an arch that holds the other stones in place. This seemed to be a fitting name, as Philadelphia eventually became the site of two Continental Congresses, and served as our nation's capital from 1790 to 1800.

From the beginning, Pennsylvania was also known for its religious tolerance. The colony was a safe haven for Quakers (Pennsylvania was later known as "The Quaker State") and other religious groups who had been persecuted in Europe.

The state is still home to the Pennsylvania Dutch, including the Amish, descendants of early German settlers. Living and worshiping much as their ancestors did, the Amish do not wear contemporary clothing, nor do they use electricity, running water, or even motorized farming equipment to till their fields. The lifestyle they enjoy in Pennsylvania is proof of the state's continued commitment to tolerance and religious freedom.

AN UNCOMMON COMMONWEALTH

The design on the back, or reverse, of one of the new quarters often represents a significant moment or person in that state's history. The woman on the back of the Pennsylvania quarter, however, represents the state itself. She is a depiction of a statue named Commonwealth that stands atop the state capitol dome in Harrisburg (a commonwealth is a group of people who are united in a common interest). If you look closely at the quarter, you will see that Commonwealth's right hand is outstretched in a gesture of mercy; in her left hand she holds a branch of ribbon mace, a symbol of justice. The words "Virtue, Liberty, and Independence"-Pennsylvania's state motto-appear to her left, and a keystone, the state's symbol, sits to her right. Together, these words and images represent the principles that Pennsylvania was founded upon.

Pennsylvania was established in 1682 by William Penn. As a young man in England, Penn rebelled against his family and upper-class society. He became a member of a religious group, the Society of Friends, also known as the Quakers, a religion that was forbidden in many places. When Penn's father died in 1670, the young man decided to use his inheritance to establish an American colony where Quakers would be free from persecution. On March 4, 1681, King Charles II signed a charter that gave William Penn a colony carved from lower New York. Penn referred to his new colony as the "holy experiment," because it was a place where people of different countries (Holland, England, Wales, and Germany, to name a few) and faiths could live and pray together in a tolerant environment. Penn was also concerned about the welfare of the Native Americans who were already living on his newly-owned land. Unlike many settlers, Penn sought a peace treaty with the local Indians, and paid them for the land that King Charles II had granted him. Penn's commitment to virtue, independence, and liberty helped shape Pennsylvania, a state whose many contributions have in turn given shape to our nation.

WHERE IT ALL BEGAN

Did you know that the decision to declare our country's independence was made in Pennsylvania? From September 5 to October 26, 1774, Philadelphia was the site of the First Continental Congress, where Patriot and Loyalist delegates from twelve of the thirteen colonies (Georgia was absent) met to discuss independence from British rule.

On May 10, 1776, the Second Continental Congress was called, after a scuffle between the British and the colonial militia (called Minutemen because of their readiness to fight at a moment's notice) left eight Minutemen dead. Because of this incident, and because of Britain's failure to meet the Patriot's other demands, the delegates decided to declare their independence from England. On July 4, 1776, they adopted and ratified the Declaration of Independence, which entitles each citizen to "life, liberty, and the pursuit of happiness." Independence Hall, the building where the famed document was drafted and signed, still stands in Philadelphia.

NOT WHAT IT'S CRACKED UP TO BE!

Have you ever wondered how the Liberty Bell in Pennsylvania got that wacky crack down its middle? The bell that has come to represent our nation's freedom was commissioned in 1751 by the Philadelphia Provincial Association, and was intended to hang in the State House (now called Independence Hall). But it cracked in a test ringing before it was ever hung. The bell was recast twice before it was finally placed in the State House, and it rang true on July 8, 1776, to commemorate the first public reading of the Declaration of Independence. During the American Revolution, the bell was hidden in a church to protect it from the British troops. Miraculously, it was never discovered. In 1846, years after its return to the State House steeple, the Liberty Bell rang for the last time, when it cracked during a celebration of George Washington's birthday.

DRINK AT YOUR OWN RISK

There is a law in Hazelton that prohibits anyone from drinking a carbonated beverage, such as soda, while teaching a class in a school auditorium.

NEW JERSEY

Capital: Trenton
State Flower: Purple Violet
State Tree: Red Oak
State Bird: Eastern Goldfinch
Land Area: 7,419 sq. mi.
Rank in Size (Land Area): 46th
State Song: "Ode to New Jersey"
Largest City: Newark
Statehood Date: December 18, 1787
Nickname: Garden State

Washington's icy trip across the Delaware River is remembered on the New Jersey quarter.

New Jersey was named in honor of Sir George Carteret, who had been governor of the island of Jersey in the English Channel.

NEW JERSEY: LIBERTY AND PROSPERITY

The area we now call New Jersey was originally inhabited by the Lenni Lenape Indians, who lived there for nearly 10,000 years. In the 1620s, Dutch settlers landed on the Jersey shore and made their way to present-day Jersey City, where they set up a trading post. By 1655, the Dutch had pushed out other settlers, and named their province "New Netherlands." However, the English eventually acquired New Jersey when King Charles II granted it to his brother James, Duke of York. But it was not until the Duke of York gave the land to Sir George Carteret and Lord John Berkeley that the colony became known as New Jersey-named after the Isle of Jersey in the English Channel.

THE GARDEN STATE

If you have ever tasted a Jersey tomato or ear of sweet Jersey corn, you would understand why New Jersey is nicknamed "The Garden State." The early colonists likened the area to a garden, because of its rich soil. In 1876, a resident of Camden called New Jersey "The Garden State," describing it as "an immense barrel, filled with good things to eat and open at both ends." Today there are more than 8,000 farms in New Jersey, and the state is a top producer of tomatoes, corn, cranberries, blueberries, peaches, eggplant, spinach, lettuce, and bell peppers.

ICY CROSSROADS

George Washington appears on both the front and back of the New Jersey quarter. On the front (obverse) is the traditional portrait that appears on all quarters, but on the back (reverse) is a picture of Washington crossing the Delaware River, headed to one of the most decisive battles of the Revolutionary War. Below this dramatic scene are the words "The Crossroads of the Revolution," because almost 100 Revolutionary War battles, took place on New Jersey soil.

In December 1776, General George Washington's troops were short of food and winter clothing, and many feared that they would not make it through the winter. But on December 13, 1776, the tide changed. American Major General Charles Lee was captured by the British, and Brigadier General John Sullivan took over Lee's troops, and marched them south to join General Washington. With 6,000 men now at his command, Washington made a critical decision that helped the colonists win the war.

The British had moved to New York, leaving a small group of Hessian mercenaries (warriors hired from Germany), in New Jersey to protect their captured land. Washington was convinced that the Hessian troops, with their British commanders so far away, would be an easy target. He also knew that if he attacked on December 26th, the Hessians would be exhausted from their Christmas festivities. In the midst of a fierce winter storm, Washington and his men boarded leaky boats and pushed their way across the nearly-frozen Delaware River. The surprise attack was a success, and the Hessians surrendered within minutes of the attack. Washington's victory in Trenton, New Jersey, was followed by the arrival of fresh troops, and eventually led to America's independence from Britain.

AN INALIENABLE RIGHT

Did you know that American women were not allowed to vote until 1920? Except for in New Jersey, that is! In 1776, a strange loophole in the law gave New Jersey women the right to vote. Women successfully cast their ballots until 1805, when male lawmakers realized the great impact of women voters on close elections. The legislators repealed women's right to vote in New Jersey, and no American woman was permitted to do it again until the ratification of the 19th Amendment to the Constitution.

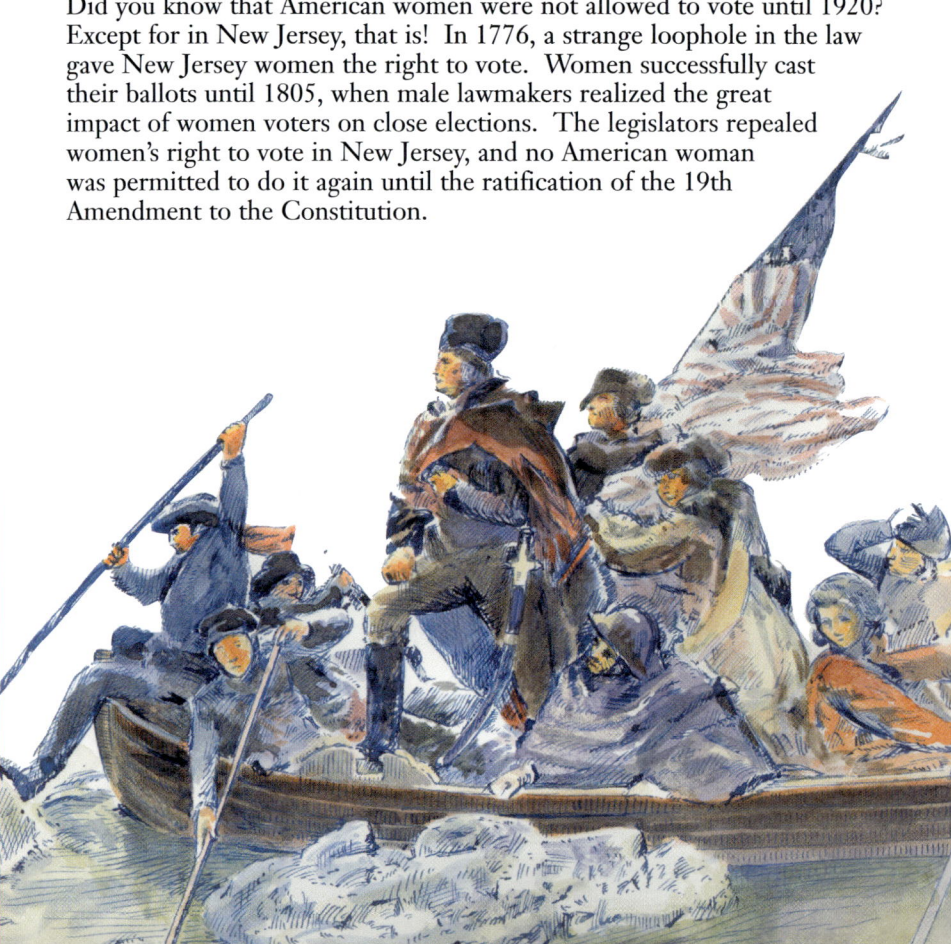

THE WIZARD OF MENLO PARK

Are you reading this with a light on? If so, you have Thomas Alva Edison to thank. An inventor with laboratories in Menlo Park and West Orange, Edison created the first carbon-filament incandescent light bulb, and also held the world record for the most patents owned by one person (a total of 1,093). Edison not only gave us light to read by, but laid the groundwork so we would have music to listen to and movies to watch. Edison's phonograph was the first machine to play recorded sounds, and he invented the apparatus that made motion pictures possible. Edison was not an ordinary genius. With only three months of formal education, he became a successful inventor by studying what interested him, and devoting all of his free time to his work. Edison proved his own theory that, "Genius is one percent inspiration, ninety-nine percent perspiration."

DINOSAUR DAYS

Most states have a state bird, insect, or tree-New Jersey has all of those things, but it also has a state dinosaur. Remains of the Hadrosaurus foulkii were first discovered in Haddonfield in 1858. The discovery of an entire dinosaur skeleton proved that dinosaurs existed, and marked the birth of paleontology, the science of studying fossils to identify ancient life forms.

EAT UP!

New Jersey is home to the most diners in the world, and is sometimes called "the diner capital of the world."

Capital: Atlanta
State Flower: Cherokee Rose
State Tree: Live Oak
State Bird: Brown Thrasher
Land Area: 57,919 sq. mi.
Rank in Size (Land Area): 21th
State Song: "Georgia On My Mind"
Largest City: Atlanta
Statehood Date: January 2, 1788
Nickname: Peach State

Georgia was named in honor of King George II of England.

Georgia's agricultural heritage is revered on the back of the state's 1999 quarter.

GEORGIA: WISDOM, JUSTICE, AND MODERATION

Georgia was named for King George II of England, who signed the colony's royal charter in 1732. Georgia is often called "The Empire State of the South," comparing it to New York City, whose nickname is "The Empire State." It is an appropriate title, considering that toward the end of the 20th century, Georgia's economy was booming and its population was growing faster than the country as a whole.

Georgia's most common nickname is "The Peach State," which refers to the state's enormous production of that fuzzy fruit. In addition to peaches, Georgia is one of the nation's largest producers of peanuts (about 800 billion a year!), lending it the nickname "The Goober State." The word goober is actually believed to come from *nguba*, an African word for peanut.

In the late 18th and early 19th centuries, African slaves were sold to plantation owners on the Sea Islands of Georgia, South Carolina, and northern Florida. Because these islands were cut off from the mainland, the slaves who lived there were isolated from mainstream culture and were able to preserve much of their African languages and traditions. Descendants of these early Africans speak a language called Gullah (from the word "Angola," where many slaves came from), which is a combination of West African, French, and English. Today, an estimated 250,000 people still speak Gullah.

WHAT A PEACH!

The large peach on the back of the Georgia quarter symbolizes its nickname, "The Peach State." The fruit is surrounded by oak branches, which represent Georgia's state tree. Some believe that the peachy nickname refers to Georgians' famously sunny disposition-but the peach also refers to Georgia's long history of agriculture, which has helped shape both the politics and economy of the state.

James Oglethorpe was granted the Georgia colony by English King George II. Oglethorpe made Georgia a physical and spiritual refuge for the poor and persecuted, where alcohol was forbidden and each family supported itself by farming the land. To prevent anyone from becoming too rich or too poor, the farmers were not allowed to own their land, and they were prohibited from using slaves to work it. With such moral laws, Georgia was the only colony of its kind. However, most of Georgia's settlers felt that they could not financially compete against other colonies without slave labor. By 1750, Georgians had successfully rallied against the colony's laws and were allowed to buy and sell land, make and sell liquor, and own slaves.

With slavery legalized, Georgia's agricultural economy prospered and the plantation system expanded. White plantation owners became rich while their African slaves toiled to harvest wheat, indigo (used as a dye), rice, and especially cotton. By 1860, four of every nine Georgians were slaves.

When slavery was abolished after the Civil War (1861-1865), the slave-dependent plantation system failed-without unpaid labor, the plantation owners could no longer cultivate cotton inexpensively. By 1890, the drop in cotton production led many farmers to diversify their crops, and the "3 Ps"- peanuts, pecans, and peaches-were introduced.

A TRUE KING

The civil rights activist Dr. Martin Luther King, Jr. (1929-1968) was born and raised in Georgia. A gifted child who began college at the age of 15, King went on to become a Baptist pastor, and in 1957 founded the Southern Christian Leadership Conference (SCLC). The SCLC was dedicated to achieving equal rights for all people through the use of non-violent tactics. To that end, King and his followers organized the March on Washington in 1963. It was during that peaceful march that King gave his famous "I have a dream" speech. The speech moved people of all races and genders to demand equal justice. In 1964, Dr. King saw the passage of the Civil Rights Act, which desegregated public places and outlawed discrimination in public facilities. That same year, he received the Nobel Peace Prize for his work, just four years before his assassination on April 4, 1968. Dr. King's contributions to his state and his country are immeasurable.

GAGA FOR GOLD

The first gold rush in North America took place in Dahlonega in 1828. *Dahlonega* is Cherokee for "yellow money," and people flocked to the area to find it. The government wanted to regulate gold mining and the use of gold currency, and in 1835 a "gold only" branch mint was established. The gold miners would drop off their gold bars, nuggets, even dust, at the mint to be melted and struck into government-certified coins. The Dahlonega Mint officially closed in May of 1861 after having been seized by Confederate forces in April 1861. In the 24 years of its operation, the Mint in Georgia produced over 1 million gold coins, some of the rarest and most valuable American coins ever made.

GIRLS ARE GREAT

As a child in Savannah in the late 19th century, Juliette Gordon Low felt that she had too many interests and not enough time to tend to them all. Inspired by the work of Lord Robert Baden-Powell, who founded the Boy Scouts in England, Juliette Gordon Low decided to start a similar program for American girls. On March 12, 1912, an eighteen-member Girl Scout troop had its first meeting, initiating an organization that eventually grew to include more than three million members.

MIND YOUR MANNERS

Gainesville is known as the Chicken Capital of the World. It is illegal to eat chicken there with a fork.

CONNECTICUT

Capital: Hartford

State Flower: Mountain Laurel

State Tree: White Oak

State Bird: Robin

Land Area: 4,845 sq. mi.

Rank in Size (Land Area): 48th

State Song: "Yankee Doodle"

Largest City: Hartford

Statehood Date: January 9, 1788

Nickname: Constitution State

The name Connecticut is based on an Indian word meaning "long river place" or "beside the long tidal river."

The Charter Oak is celebrated on the Connecticut quarter.

CONNECTICUT: HE WHO TRANSPLANTS STILL SUSTAINS

When Connecticut was first settled by Europeans in 1633, it was inhabited by several Native American tribes, including the Mohawk, Mohegan, and Pequot. These peoples referred to their land as "Quinnehukgut," meaning "beside the long tidal river." The Europeans adopted this name and changed it slightly, calling their colony "Connecticut."

In 1638, Connecticut's colonists made history when they drafted the "Fundamental Orders." These were a set of laws that organized the colonial government very much like the U.S. Constitution established the American government. Because many historians consider the Orders to be the first constitution ever written, Connecticut is nicknamed the "The Constitution State."

Connecticut is sometimes referred to as "The Provisions State," a name it acquired during the American Revolution, when Connecticut provided most of the food and cannons to the Continental Army. It has also been called "The Nutmeg State," based on the fragrant spice sold by Yankee peddlers. There is a story that Connecticut peddlers were so crafty that they made and sold wooden nutmegs to unsuspecting buyers. As Connecticut's many names reveal, the state has a vivid and fascinating history.

THE ROOT OF OUR INDEPENDENCE

On the back of Connecticut's quarter is the Charter Oak, a majestic tree whose story changed the future of Connecticut and America.

When the colony of Connecticut was formed in 1639, it was a combination of the Hartford, Wethersfield, and Windsor settlements. To ensure that each settlement and every colonist would be fairly represented, settlement representatives met to discuss the drafting of a set of basic laws. On January 14, the colonists adopted the Fundamental Orders, a framework of laws that provided for a self-governing colony. Settlement leaders, such as Thomas Hooker of Hartford, felt strongly that people should be allowed to vote directly for their representatives and to limit the representatives' power. Much like our Constitution calls for Congress and the Supreme Court, the Fundamental Orders established two general assemblies-one was legislative, and the other judicial.

Under the new laws, Connecticut was the only colony allowed to appoint its own governor, rather than be ruled by an officer of the King. Connecticut (and the New Haven colony it absorbed) prospered until Sir Edmond Andros, the governor of the Dominion of New England, attempted to stake a claim on the colony. When Sir Edmund charged into the Hartford capital in 1687, he demanded that the Connecticut government hand over its charter. During a heated argument between Sir Edmund and government officials, all the candles in the room suddenly went out. When they were re-lit, the charter had disappeared.

Connecticut's royal charter was hidden in a massive white oak tree which came to be known as The Charter Oak, and stands as a symbol of Connecticut's, and our country's, struggle for independence. The mighty oak stood tall until it was felled by a storm in 1856.

THAR SHE BLOWS!

Try saying *Physeter macrocephalus* three times, fast! That is the Latin name for the sperm whale, designated Connecticut's state whale in 1975. In the 19th century, the whaling industry was very important to Connecticut's economy. Americans used whale products like oil, bones, and a waxy substance called ambergris, to light their lamps, stiffen their corsets, and make perfume. Connecticut whalers traveled the globe hunting the animal. Eventually, this took a terrible toll on the sperm whale population, which is now on the endangered species list.

HAVE A HEART
In 1982, a Stamford native, Dr. Robert K. Jarvik, invented the world's first artificial heart. A small machine made from plastic, metal, and polyester, the Jarvik-7 works by pushing blood from one part of the heart into the other through a system of pressurized air hoses. Jarvik's invention was the first step toward keeping heart patients alive when a transplant was not possible. When first used in 1982, the machine kept a patient alive for 112 miraculous days.

PRUDENCE THE PERSISTENT
In 1833, Prudence Crandall founded the first school in New England for African-American women. For nearly 18 months, Crandall stood tall against those who opposed education for African-Americans. She was arrested and tried twice for refusing to close her academy. Although the charges against Crandall eventually were dropped, the school was threatened by mob violence and shut its doors in 1834. Crandall's achievements were finally recognized in 1886, when the Connecticut state legislature awarded her with an annual pension of $400.

PLEASE PASS THE PIE
The disc-throwing game we call "Frisbee" was invented in New Haven. In 1920, some students from Yale University decided to see what happened when they tossed around an empty pie plate from Mrs. Frisbie's pie company. The dish flew, and the game of Frisbee was born.

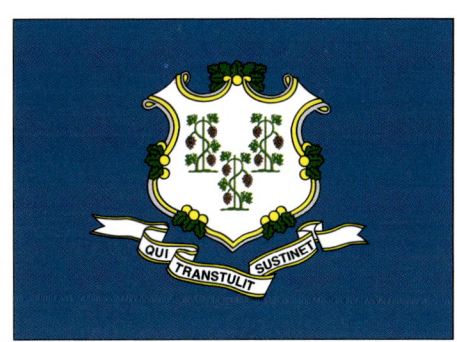

LOOK MA, NO HANDS!
In Hartford, Connecticut, no one may cross the street on his or her hands.

PROGRAM

Founded by an act of Congress on April 2, 1792, the United States Mint has been operating for more than 200 years. The Mint produces between 14 and 20 billion circulating coins annually, as well as gold, silver, and platinum coins, proof coins and medals.

The first Mint was constructed in Philadelphia, Pennsylvania. Coins have been produced at this location since 1793. Since this was our only mint for many years, no mint mark was used until 1979 (except on 1942-1945 nickels). Still today the absence of a mint mark designates a coin as a product of the Philadelphia Mint, although a few coins including the quarters of the 50 State Quarters™ Program series do include a "P" mint mark. All engraving for U.S. coins is done at the Philadelphia Mint.

The Philadelphia Mint was our only mint until 1838 when the Dahlonega, Georgia (gold coins only), Charlotte, North Carolina (gold coins only), and New Orleans, Louisiana, mints were established. Later, the Carson City, Denver, San Francisco and West Point mints were created.

For more information about the U.S. Mint, visit www.USMINT.gov.